Table of Contents

INTRODUCTION

In a world filled with ever-changing trends, algorithms, and new digital marketing tools popping up every other day, it's easy to get lost in the chaos. The pressure to be innovative, the obsession with optimization, and the constant need to stay on top of the latest buzzwords can make any marketer feel like they're drowning in a sea of complexities. But here's the thing—amid all the noise, there's one simple truth that often gets overlooked: **Common sense is the secret weapon in digital marketing.**

The industry is constantly evolving, and while keeping up with new technologies and strategies is important, it's even more crucial to remember the foundational principles that have stood the test of time. These are the principles that form the backbone of any successful marketing campaign: understanding your audience, making simple decisions based on logic, and building meaningful relationships that transcend the digital noise. Unfortunately, in our quest for innovation, we often forget that these fundamentals are the keys to long-term success.

"Beyond the Buzzwords: Applying Common Sense in Digital Marketing" is here to remind you of that. This book isn't about mastering the latest software, riding the next big trend, or using marketing jargon to sound impressive. Instead, it's about bringing things back to basics and showing you how applying common sense can elevate your marketing efforts, no matter how small or large your business may be.

In each chapter, we'll break down complex concepts and strategies and give them a no-nonsense, practical approach. We'll talk about how to make smarter decisions, how to avoid falling for the hype, and how to craft campaigns that resonate with your audience because, at the end of the day, your success as a marketer relies on creating real, meaningful connections—not on using the most advanced tools or following the latest trend.

We'll explore real-world examples, share actionable tips, and even throw in a few lighthearted moments to keep things fun. After all, marketing is supposed to be creative, engaging, and—most importantly—human.

So if you're tired of overcomplicating things, if you want to cut through the jargon and start focusing on what really works, then this book is for you. We're about to embark on a journey of practical wisdom, where common sense leads the way to better campaigns, higher conversions, and stronger customer relationships. Let's ditch the buzzwords, embrace simplicity, and get to work on marketing that makes sense.

Ready? Let's dive in.

CHAPTER 1: THE ROLE OF COMMON SENSE IN DIGITAL MARKETING

Defining Common Sense in Marketing

Let's be real. Digital marketing is full of jargon, trends, and buzzwords that are enough to make anyone's head spin. But here's the secret—none of that matters if you don't have one thing: common sense.

In digital marketing, common sense is the backbone of every successful strategy. It's the practical decision-making process that guides everything you do. Instead of blindly following the latest fad or overcomplicating things with buzzwords like "synergy" or "disruptive innovation" (seriously, who actually knows what that means?), common sense focuses on simple, logical steps that help connect you with your audience in a meaningful way.

Think about it this way: Would you trust a company that can't make a simple decision, like designing a logo that actually looks good, or writing a website copy that doesn't sound like it was auto-generated by a robot? Of course not! Common sense in marketing isn't just about understanding your audience; it's about taking that understanding and translating it into strategies that work. And spoiler alert: it's not rocket science.

So, what exactly does common sense in digital marketing look like? It's making sure your brand's identity makes sense and aligns with what your audience cares about. It's ensuring that your website is easy to navigate. It's crafting an email campaign that doesn't come off as an automated sales pitch (because who even reads those anymore?). It's about taking action based on clear, simple insights rather than jumping on the latest shiny object.

Why It's Overlooked

Now, here's the thing. Common sense is often the first thing that gets pushed to the backburner in the digital marketing world. Why? Because there's a never-ending pressure to be "innovative" and "cutting-edge." As if throwing around words like "disruptive" or "game-changing" will automatically make you a marketing genius.

But let's face it—this obsession with "new" can be distracting. Too often, marketing professionals end up chasing the latest trends, buying into the next big tech tool, or attempting to integrate every platform under the sun without actually stopping to ask: "Does this even make sense for my audience? Is this the best approach for my brand?"

Here's the catch: The truth is, marketers often think the more complex and high-tech something is, the better it is. So, they load their campaigns with tons of features, processes, and sophisticated tools, all in an effort to seem cutting-edge. But sometimes, all that complexity does is confuse both the marketer and the audience.

For instance, when was the last time you read an email marketing campaign that felt human, rather than robotic? Or when was the last time you saw a website that was so easy to navigate, you didn't even realize you were on it for 30 minutes? That's common sense at work.

But Why Does It Matter?

Because when common sense is the foundation, everything else falls into place naturally. If your marketing strategy is based on understanding your audience's needs, wants, and behaviors, you're already ahead of the game. This isn't about building the flashiest campaign or leveraging every tech tool in the market. It's about being authentic, clear, and user-centered.

The Trap of Over-Automation

You know what they say about too much of a good thing, right? Well, the same goes for automation in digital marketing. Don't get me wrong—automation is a great tool. It can save time, help you streamline processes, and manage campaigns more efficiently. But here's where the trap lies: it can also be a shortcut to laziness if you're not careful.

How many times have you seen an automated email sequence that starts off well but then gradually loses its relevance, humor, or personal touch? Or an ad campaign that's optimized so much, it's no longer even relatable to real people? Automated systems can work wonders, but they can also make your marketing feel sterile and disconnected from the human touch that builds trust.

And trust, my friend, is everything in digital marketing. Without common sense, you can easily fall into the trap of thinking that because something works on paper, it'll automatically work in real life. Spoiler alert: it won't.

Innovation Without Fundamentals

Let's talk about the whole "innovative" thing for a second. You've probably heard someone say, "We need to innovate! We need to be ahead of the curve!" But, here's a little truth bomb for you: **Innovation without a solid foundation is just chaos.**

Yes, new tech and strategies are important, but if you're jumping into them without understanding the fundamentals— like audience behavior, content quality, and clear communication —your innovation will only add confusion to the mix. It's like trying to build a house on a shaky foundation: no matter how cool your blueprint looks, the house will eventually crumble.

Example: Remember when people were obsessed with AI chatbots a few years ago? Sure, they sounded cool and futuristic, but many brands rushed into using them without really thinking through their execution. The result? A bunch of frustrated customers talking to robots that couldn't understand anything beyond basic questions.

Common sense here would have been to first ensure that their human-centered support experience was rock-solid before jumping into AI.

Lack of Real-World Experience

Sometimes, marketers who are fresh out of school or have only been in the industry for a short time lean too heavily on theory and trends, overlooking real-world applications. Let's be honest: theory is important, but real-world experience teaches you one crucial thing: **what actually works.**

Real-world marketing often involves trial and error, adjusting strategies based on feedback, and using common sense to know when something just isn't working. It's understanding that not every tool or strategy is a one-size-fits-all solution. Marketing is messy, and that's perfectly fine.

How to Bring Common Sense Back to the Table

Here's the good news: common sense is something you can develop, practice, and apply. And here's how you do it:

1. **Start with the Basics**: Focus on understanding your audience first, not on the latest trend. Be real with them. If they're tired of long-form blog posts, don't force one down their throats.
2. **Simplify, Don't Overcomplicate**: Sure, technology can be great, but don't use a hammer when a screwdriver will do the job. Stick with what's simple and effective.
3. **Stay Focused on the Human Element**: Remember that digital marketing is ultimately about people. If your campaigns aren't resonating with real humans, it doesn't matter how many analytics tools you use or how much data you gather.

4. **Embrace Flexibility**: Digital marketing isn't about rigid systems; it's about agility. Sometimes common sense means knowing when to switch gears or scrap an idea altogether.

Conclusion: Common Sense is Your Secret Weapon

In the end, the secret to successful digital marketing isn't buried in a fancy new algorithm or hidden behind a wall of buzzwords. It's simply about being logical, empathetic, and focused on the basics. Embrace common sense, and you'll be miles ahead of the curve.

So, the next time you find yourself tangled in a web of digital marketing lingo, take a deep breath and ask yourself: Does this make sense? If it does, you're on the right track. If not, maybe it's time to go back to the drawing board—and leave the buzzwords at the door.

CHAPTER 2: UNDERSTANDING YOUR AUDIENCE

Personas vs. Genuine Connections

If you've been in digital marketing for any amount of time, you've probably heard about audience personas. They're the detailed, often overly specific profiles marketers create to represent their ideal customers. These personas include everything from demographic information to preferences, hobbies, and purchasing behavior. And don't get me wrong, creating personas can be a useful exercise when starting out, but there's one thing that's often overlooked: **personas don't always lead to genuine connections.**

Here's the deal: personas are great for mapping out broad trends and generalizing about your audience, but they don't capture the complexity of real human beings. Humans are not just statistics or a list of traits. We're emotional, unpredictable, and multi-dimensional. If you rely solely on a set of data points to guide your marketing efforts, you might end up missing out on the deeper connections that drive brand loyalty and long-term engagement.

A persona might tell you that your audience is mostly women, aged 25-35, who love yoga and live in urban areas. But it doesn't tell you about how they feel after a stressful day or what really motivates them to buy a product or sign up for a service. That's where the magic of **genuine connections** comes into play.

True audience understanding goes beyond the numbers. It's about getting into their heads, speaking their language, and, most importantly, relating to their emotions. The more you understand the real people behind the data, the better equipped you'll be to create marketing that resonates on a personal level.

Avoiding Missteps

There's one thing every marketer has to remember when dealing with human beings: we're all different. This means that failing to account for the diversity of your audience can result in campaigns that are tone-deaf, irrelevant, or even offensive. As marketers, we need to be extra careful not to make the mistake of assuming that "everyone" thinks, behaves, or feels the same way. That's where things can go horribly wrong.

Let's start with the most basic mistake: **ignoring cultural differences.** Imagine running a campaign in India where your content features humor that might be funny to your Western audience but is completely lost—or worse, offensive—to your Indian customers. This can happen when marketers assume a universal appeal without considering the diverse backgrounds, beliefs, and values of their audience. Common sense here? Know your audience's culture, values, and context. Otherwise, your campaign will be more of a headache than a hit.

Another misstep is **misreading your audience's tone**. Picture this: you're selling a relaxation product aimed at stressed-out professionals. You decide to run a campaign using humor that feels a little too cheeky, making light of their anxiety. While some may laugh it off, many will find it distasteful, dismissive, and totally out of touch with their reality. People don't like being laughed at or made to feel like their pain is just a joke.

Common sense here? Treat your audience with respect, empathy, and sensitivity. Understand where they're coming from, and communicate with them in a way that acknowledges their unique experiences and emotions. Authenticity goes a long way in building trust.

Listening to Your Audience (The Right Way)

Understanding your audience is a continuous, evolving process. You can't just set up a persona once and forget about it. You need to constantly listen to your customers, paying attention to their feedback, concerns, and desires. This doesn't mean just looking at analytics reports or survey results—it means really listening.

Have you ever been part of a focus group or customer review session where the feedback completely blindsided you? That's because, while data can tell you a lot about what people do, it doesn't always reveal **why** they do it. Why did they abandon their cart? Why did they sign up for your newsletter? What makes them choose one brand over another? Asking these questions and truly listening to the answers is where the gold lies.

You can start by tracking conversations on social media, reading customer reviews, and asking direct questions through surveys or emails. Then, take that feedback and use it to adjust your approach. If your audience wants more in-depth content, give it to them. If they want more personalization, make it happen. If they're asking for a solution to a pain point, stop pitching and start solving.

Listening isn't just about collecting data; it's about interpreting it in a way that enhances your connection with your audience. A genuine connection can only happen when you know your audience so well that you're able to predict their needs and desires before they even have to voice them.

Building Trust Through Transparency

One of the biggest keys to building lasting connections with your audience is **trust**. In an age where consumers are more skeptical than ever, being transparent and honest in your marketing is non-negotiable. People can smell inauthenticity from a mile away. And if your audience feels like you're just another brand trying to sell them something, they'll quickly tune out.

Trust starts with being upfront about your intentions. If you're promoting a product, don't oversell it. Be honest about what it does and, more importantly, what it doesn't do. If your company made a mistake, own up to it. Acknowledge issues, explain how you're fixing them, and keep your audience updated. This approach builds credibility over time, showing your audience that you're not just out to make a quick sale—you're in it for the long haul.

Common sense here? People value honesty, and they can see through a sales pitch that's all fluff and no substance. So be real. Be transparent. And most importantly, be **consistent** in the messages you send out.

Creating Content That Speaks to Your Audience

Once you understand your audience and have built a level of trust, the next step is creating content that truly speaks to them. Content isn't just about filling space on your website or social media pages; it's about giving your audience something valuable that they want to engage with. Whether that's a blog post, video, podcast, or social media update, make sure your content is aligned with your audience's needs and interests.

Start by putting yourself in your audience's shoes. What do they care about? What keeps them up at night? What's their biggest challenge? Address those issues directly in your content.

Here's a fun thought experiment: imagine your ideal customer sitting across from you in a coffee shop. What would you say to them? What would they ask you? If you can answer those questions, you've got the foundation for some seriously engaging content.

And remember, it's not just about talking *to* your audience; it's about engaging *with* them. Use your content to encourage interaction—ask questions, start conversations, and invite feedback. Your audience will appreciate it, and you'll start to build a community of loyal followers who feel heard and valued.

Conclusion: The Human Touch

In the end, understanding your audience isn't about collecting a bunch of numbers and statistics—it's about creating a genuine connection with real people. If you can tap into their emotions, understand their needs, and communicate with them authentically, you'll have a far more effective marketing strategy than any set of personas could ever provide.

So, ditch the stereotypes, toss out the assumptions, and start listening. Because once you truly understand your audience, you'll be in the best position to create marketing campaigns that speak directly to them—and that's where the real magic happens.

CHAPTER 3: BUILDING A STRONG DIGITAL IDENTITY

In the crowded digital marketplace, establishing a strong and recognizable digital identity isn't just a nice-to-have—it's a must. Your brand is more than just a logo or a color scheme; it's a reflection of your values, your story, and the experience you promise to deliver. Without a clear and consistent digital identity, your audience won't know who you are, what you stand for, or why they should care. So, how do you build an identity that's not only memorable but also authentic? Let's dive in.

The Power of a Simple, Memorable Logo

Let's start with the most obvious component of your digital identity: your logo. The logo is often the first thing people will see when they come across your brand, so it's essential to get it right. But here's the catch—**simple is better**.

A good logo is memorable, scalable, and easily recognizable. Think about the golden arches of McDonald's, the swoosh of Nike, or the apple of Apple. These logos are simple, and they stick in your mind because they don't try to do too much. The mistake that many businesses make is over-complicating their logos with intricate designs, confusing shapes, or too many colors.

The trick to a great logo is keeping it clean and straightforward while ensuring it aligns with your brand's values. Whether you're a tech startup, a yoga studio, or a restaurant, your logo should communicate what your brand is all about. For example, a logo for a wellness brand might feature earthy tones and smooth curves to convey tranquility and balance. A tech company, on the other hand, might opt for sharp lines and bold colors to communicate innovation and precision.

Common sense tip: Remember, your logo doesn't have to tell your whole brand story. It's an emblem—something that visually represents who you are, not the entire encyclopedia of your brand. Less is often more.

The Importance of Consistency Across Platforms

Once you've nailed your logo, it's time to take a look at your brand's overall visual identity. Consistency is key here. Whether someone is looking at your website, scrolling through your social media feed, or seeing your ads on Google, every touchpoint should feel like it belongs to the same brand. This creates a seamless experience and helps build brand recognition.

Imagine walking into a store where the signage looks completely different from the staff uniforms, and the website is a completely different color scheme. How likely are you to trust that brand? Not very likely, right? The same principle applies to your digital presence.

A consistent visual identity includes things like:

- **Color palette**: Choose a few primary colors that reflect your brand's personality and use them across all your marketing materials.
- **Typography**: Select one or two fonts that are easy to read and reflect your brand's tone.
- **Imagery**: Use images that align with your brand's message and keep a similar style across platforms. No random stock photos, please.

In addition to visual consistency, make sure your brand voice is unified. Whether your tone is professional, friendly, witty, or authoritative, it should be consistent across all communication channels.

Common sense tip: Think of your brand as a person. Would you trust someone who constantly changed their personality depending on the situation? Probably not. Your brand should be the same person across all platforms—approachable, trustworthy, and consistent.

Crafting a Compelling Brand Story

Your digital identity isn't just about how you look; it's also about who you are. What's your story? Why does your brand exist, and how do you solve problems for your audience? People don't buy products—they buy **stories** and experiences. A compelling brand story can set you apart from competitors and create an emotional connection with your audience.

Your story should answer key questions:

- **Why did your brand start?** What problem were you trying to solve?
- **What values guide your brand?** What do you stand for beyond selling products?
- **What's your mission?** What do you want to accomplish, and how will you make a difference?

Once you've answered these questions, you need to communicate your story clearly. Use your website, social media profiles, and email newsletters to tell your brand's tale. Don't just say, "We sell amazing products"; say, "We believe in making your life easier by providing products that solve real problems, backed by exceptional service." Make your audience feel like they're part of something bigger.

Common sense tip: A good story doesn't need to be a dramatic novel. Be genuine, be human, and focus on what matters most to your audience. No one cares about your 30-page backstory unless it speaks to them.

Business Naming: Get It Right From the Start

Choosing the right name for your business may seem like a small detail, but it's a big deal. Your business name is the foundation of your brand, and it can impact everything from your logo design to your SEO ranking. A good name should be:

- **Memorable**: Easy to say, spell, and remember. Think of names like Google, Nike, or Tesla. They're short, snappy, and unforgettable.
- **Relevant**: The name should reflect the essence of your business and be aligned with your brand's purpose.
- **Unique**: Avoid names that sound too generic or are easily confused with existing businesses. You don't want your brand to get lost in a sea of similar-sounding names.

It's also crucial to check whether your desired business name is available as a domain and across social media platforms. Having consistency across your online presence is important for branding and SEO purposes.

Common sense tip: A business name is your brand's first impression, so make it count. If it's too complicated, people won't remember it. If it's too generic, people won't notice it. Get the balance right, and you're off to a great start.

The Role of Digital Identity in Building Trust

Your digital identity isn't just about looking good—it's about building **trust** with your audience. A professional, cohesive digital identity conveys that you're serious about what you do and that you care about the details. If your website looks outdated, your logo looks like a five-year-old designed it, and your social media feed is all over the place, your audience is going to wonder if you're actually credible.

Trust is the foundation of every successful customer relationship. People need to believe that your business is reliable, authentic, and capable of delivering on its promises. By creating a strong, consistent, and professional digital identity, you're telling your audience, "We know what we're doing, and we're here to stay."

Common sense tip: First impressions matter. If your digital identity feels off or inconsistent, people will doubt your ability to deliver. So take the time to get it right and keep it professional.

Conclusion: Your Digital Identity is Your Brand's First Impression

Building a strong digital identity is an ongoing process, but it's also one of the most important things you can do for your business. Your brand's identity tells the world who you are, what you stand for, and why you matter. It sets the tone for every interaction and lays the foundation for building trust, loyalty, and recognition.

So take a step back, look at your current digital identity, and ask yourself: Does it reflect the essence of my brand? Is it consistent across all platforms? Does it resonate with my audience? If the answer is no, it's time for a refresh. A strong digital identity is your first step toward a successful and enduring brand.

CHAPTER 4:
WEBSITE DESIGN
WITH PURPOSE

In the age of digital interactions, your website is often the first and most important touchpoint between you and your audience. It's your brand's home on the internet, a place where people should feel welcome, informed, and motivated to take action. Yet, despite how critical websites are to business success, many companies miss the mark when it comes to creating a site that truly serves both the user and the brand. A website that's clunky, hard to navigate, or outdated won't just frustrate visitors—it can actively drive them away.

But fear not! This chapter will guide you through the basics of building a website that doesn't just look good, but also performs well. The key? **Purposeful design** that focuses on user experience (UX), clear calls-to-action (CTAs), and mobile optimization. Oh, and yes—don't forget to add a sprinkle of common sense along the way!

User Experience (UX): The Heart of Good Website Design

User experience (UX) is all about how a visitor interacts with your website. It's the difference between a seamless, enjoyable experience and one that makes people want to throw their laptop out the window. UX design focuses on making the user's journey as smooth and intuitive as possible, which ultimately leads to better conversions and customer satisfaction.

A website with great UX ensures that visitors can find what they need quickly, without unnecessary clicks or frustration. This includes clear navigation, fast loading times, and an overall layout that feels familiar and easy to understand. Let's break this down:

- **Navigation**: Keep the navigation simple and logical. A visitor shouldn't have to hunt for your contact page, product listings, or blog. Organize your site so that information is easy to find and categorize, and consider a sticky menu that follows visitors as they scroll.

- **Clear Structure**: People don't like clutter. Stick to a clean, minimalist layout where important information stands out. Too many buttons or text-heavy pages can overwhelm visitors. A well-structured site helps guide users where they need to go without making them feel lost.

- **Consistency**: Just like with your brand's visual identity, your website should maintain a consistent style. This includes colors, fonts, and button placements. Consistency helps with both usability and recognition, making your website feel more like a natural extension of your brand.

Common sense tip: If someone lands on your website and has to squint to find the navigation bar or gets confused about where to click next, you're already in trouble. Keep it simple. Keep it intuitive.

The Importance of Fast Load Times

Nobody likes waiting, and that includes waiting for a website to load. Research shows that people are incredibly impatient when it comes to websites, with most expecting a site to load in **under 3 seconds**. If your site is sluggish or takes too long to load, visitors will likely abandon it, and that means lost opportunities for conversions.

There are a few common culprits when it comes to slow websites:

- **Large, unoptimized images**: Big images can take forever to load, especially if they're not compressed or resized to the right dimensions.
- **Too many plugins or widgets**: While plugins can enhance functionality, they can also slow your site down if there are too many running at once.
- **Overloaded web hosting**: If your website is hosted on a server that's too slow or overcrowded, your site's speed will suffer.

Common sense tip: Test your website's speed regularly using tools like Google's PageSpeed Insights or GTmetrix. If it's slow, it's time to optimize.

Clear Call-to-Actions (CTAs): Directing Visitors to Take Action

Imagine you're walking through a store. You've found what you're looking for, and now you need to check out. But wait—there's no clear register, no signage telling you where to go, and no one to assist you. Frustrating, right? This is what happens when a website lacks clear calls-to-action (CTAs).

A CTA is a prompt on your website that encourages visitors to take a specific action, whether it's subscribing to a newsletter, purchasing a product, or downloading a free resource. It's how you guide visitors down the path to conversion. Without effective CTAs, your website becomes a maze where users don't know what to do next.

Here's how to get CTAs right:

- **Be clear and concise**: Your CTA should use action-oriented language that clearly states what you want the user to do. "Buy Now," "Get Started," "Sign Up," and "Learn More" are all great examples.

- **Stand out visually**: Your CTA should stand out on the page.

Use bold colors that contrast with your website's background and place the button in a location where it's easy to find (like near the top of the page or at the end of a section).

- **Offer value**: Give users a reason to click. "Sign up for a free trial" or "Download your free eBook" are much more enticing than simply "Subscribe." Focus on the benefit users will receive by taking action.

Common sense tip: If your website visitors don't know where to go next, or if they get distracted by a dozen competing buttons, you've failed to guide them. Make your CTAs clear, direct, and prominent.

Mobile Optimization: Why It's Non-Negotiable

We live in a mobile-first world, where people are just as likely to browse the internet on their phones as they are on their desktops. In fact, **over 50% of global web traffic** comes from mobile devices. If your website isn't optimized for mobile, you're missing out on a huge chunk of potential customers.

Here's what mobile optimization should look like:

- **Responsive Design**: Your website should automatically adjust its layout depending on the screen size. A good responsive design ensures that your website looks great on everything from a smartphone to a tablet to a desktop.

- **Easy-to-Tap Buttons**: On mobile devices, users are navigating with their fingers, not a mouse. This means buttons, links, and CTAs should be large enough to tap easily without zooming in.

- **Readability**: Text should be large enough to read on a small screen, and the layout should avoid horizontal scrolling. No one likes having to zoom in on a mobile website to see the text properly.

Common sense tip: Test your website on multiple devices to make sure it's user-friendly on mobile. If it's not, you're turning away a large number of potential visitors.

The Role of Visual Content in Website Design

Websites aren't just about functionality—they're also about **engagement**. One of the best ways to keep visitors engaged and increase the likelihood of conversion is through **visual content**. High-quality images, videos, and graphics add visual appeal and communicate your brand's message in a more dynamic and engaging way than text alone.

But remember, the visuals you use should always serve a purpose. Don't load your website with unnecessary stock photos or cluttered designs. Choose visuals that align with your brand's identity and message. A clean, well-organized website with a few strategic images or videos will always outperform a cluttered site with random pictures everywhere.

Common sense tip: Don't overload your site with visuals just for the sake of it. Each image or video should have a clear purpose and align with your brand's goals.

Conclusion: Designing with Purpose for Results

Designing a website is like building a house—it needs a solid foundation, a clear structure, and careful thought about how people will move through the space. A website with purpose-driven design will not only make visitors feel welcome and informed but will also guide them to take the actions you want them to take. By focusing on user experience, fast load times, clear CTAs, mobile optimization, and visual content, you'll build a website that's both functional and enjoyable.

In the next chapter, we'll dig into the science of keyword research —because if no one can find your beautiful website, what's the point of building it?

CHAPTER 5: THE ART OF KEYWORD RESEARCH

Imagine you've spent hours crafting the perfect blog post. You've written engaging content, added a few high-quality images, and even sprinkled in a few jokes to keep things light. You publish it, sit back, and wait for the views to roll in. But... nothing. Crickets. Your blog post is buried somewhere on the internet, unseen and unloved. Why? Because you forgot the most important thing: **keywords**.

Keywords are the bridge between what people are searching for and the content you're creating. They are the terms and phrases that users type into search engines when looking for information. And let's face it: if you don't show up in those search results, it doesn't matter how good your content is. Without the right keywords, your content might as well be invisible.

But don't worry, you don't have to be a keyword wizard to get it right. In this chapter, we'll walk through the basics of keyword research, how to apply it strategically, and how to avoid common mistakes that even seasoned marketers make. Ready to ensure your content gets the attention it deserves? Let's dive in.

Knowing Your Audience's Search Intent

Before you even start looking for keywords, you need to understand **search intent**—the reason behind a user's search query. Search intent can be broken down into three main categories:

1. **Informational**: The user is looking for information. For example, someone might search for "how to tie a tie" or "what is SEO."

2. **Navigational**: The user is looking for a specific website or brand. For example, "Facebook login" or "Nike official site."

3. **Transactional**: The user is ready to make a purchase or take some sort of action. For example, "buy iPhone 13" or "best yoga mat for beginners."

When doing keyword research, it's crucial to match your content with the correct search intent. Why? Because if someone is searching for how to make banana bread (informational) and your page is selling banana bread mixes (transactional), they're not likely to convert. You've got to give them what they want when they search for it.

Common sense tip: Don't just chase high-volume keywords. Focus on keywords that match the intent behind the search. Aligning your content with the user's expectations will lead to better results.

Short-Tail vs. Long-Tail Keywords

When doing keyword research, you'll come across two main types of keywords: **short-tail** and **long-tail**.

- **Short-tail keywords**: These are broad, one or two-word phrases like "digital marketing" or "fitness." They often have high search volume, but they're also highly competitive. Ranking for these keywords is a long shot, especially if you're just starting out.

- **Long-tail keywords**: These are longer, more specific

phrases, such as "best digital marketing strategies for small businesses" or "how to lose weight with yoga for beginners." While these have lower search volume, they tend to be less competitive, and they often attract users with a clear intent to take action.

Long-tail keywords are especially valuable because they target a more qualified audience. People searching for long-tail terms are often further along in the buying cycle and are more likely to convert.

Common sense tip: Don't just go after the big, flashy short-tail keywords. Find long-tail gems that are specific to your audience's needs. They might not get as many searches, but they can drive higher-quality traffic.

Using Tools to Discover Keywords

There are plenty of tools out there that can help you find keywords that match your content. Some of the most popular options include:

- **Google Keyword Planner**: This free tool from Google allows you to see keyword volume, competition, and related keyword ideas. It's great for getting a sense of what's popular in your industry.

- **SEMrush**: This tool is fantastic for competitor analysis. It lets you see which keywords your competitors are ranking for, so you can identify gaps in your own strategy.

- **Ahrefs**: Known for its backlink analysis, Ahrefs also has a powerful keyword research tool that provides keyword difficulty scores and search volume estimates.

- **Ubersuggest**: This tool is great for finding long-tail keywords and provides a variety of keyword suggestions based on your main search term.

These tools can help you build a keyword list, but remember: **don't just rely on the data.** Use your own knowledge of your audience and industry to refine your keyword choices.

Common sense tip: Tools are helpful, but they're just tools. Don't make the mistake of blindly following the data. Think about what your audience is actually searching for and how they'll interact with your content.

Strategic Keyword Application

Once you've gathered your list of keywords, it's time to integrate them into your content. But hold on! Don't just sprinkle keywords all over your page like confetti. That's called **keyword stuffing**, and it's about as effective as throwing spaghetti at the wall to see what sticks. Instead, you should focus on **strategic placement**. Here's how:

1. **Title Tag**: This is one of the most important places to include your target keyword. A well-crafted title tag can significantly improve your chances of ranking.

2. **Meta Description**: While the meta description doesn't directly impact rankings, it does play a role in whether people click on your result. Include your primary keyword here and make sure the description is engaging.

3. **Headings (H1, H2, H3)**: Use your keywords naturally in the headings. This helps both search engines and users understand the structure and relevance of your content.

4. **Body Content**: Integrate keywords naturally throughout your content. Aim for quality and readability, not forced keyword use. Your content should flow logically and provide real value to the

reader.

5. **Alt Text for Images**: Use descriptive alt text for your images and include keywords where appropriate. This helps search engines understand what the images are about and can boost your rankings for image searches.

Common sense tip: Don't overdo it. Use keywords where they make sense, but prioritize creating content that's useful, engaging, and easy to read. Google is smart—it knows when you're trying to game the system.

Avoiding Keyword Stuffing and Other Pitfalls

Keyword stuffing is one of the most common mistakes people make during SEO. It involves cramming as many keywords as possible into your content in an attempt to rank higher. But search engines have evolved, and they can now detect and penalize keyword stuffing. Instead of ranking higher, your content could be demoted in the search results.

- **Keyword Stuffing**: This happens when you overuse keywords, making the content sound unnatural or awkward.

- **Ignoring Search Intent**: As mentioned earlier, you need to match keywords with the user's intent. Don't just chase keywords because they're popular—ensure they're relevant to what the user is looking for.

- **Focusing Too Much on SEO**: While keywords are important, they shouldn't be the sole focus of your content. Don't sacrifice readability and engagement for the sake of optimization. Google values high-quality, user-focused content.

Common sense tip: Keep the focus on the user. Write for your audience, not for search engines. SEO is important, but it's just one piece of the puzzle.

Conclusion: The Keyword Dance

Keyword research isn't just about finding words with the highest search volume. It's about understanding your audience, aligning with their search intent, and integrating keywords naturally into content that's valuable and engaging.

By using the right tools, focusing on both short-tail and long-tail keywords, and applying them strategically, you'll be able to drive more qualified traffic to your site and improve your chances of ranking higher in search results.

In the next chapter, we'll explore how to create visual content that resonates with your audience. Because let's face it: in today's digital world, a picture (or a video) is worth a thousand words—and we've got to make those words count!

CHAPTER 6: CREATING VISUAL CONTENT THAT SPEAKS

Picture this: You're scrolling through your social media feed, and something catches your eye. Maybe it's a vibrant image, an intriguing video, or a funny meme. Whatever it is, it's visually compelling, and it stops you in your tracks. You pause, engage, and maybe even share it with your friends. That, my friend, is the power of **visual content**.

In the fast-paced digital world we live in, where attention spans are shorter than ever, visual content is no longer just a luxury —it's a necessity. People process images 60,000 times faster than text, and research shows that content with visuals gets 94% more views than content without visuals. If you want your marketing to stand out, you need to integrate visuals that are not only eye-catching but also relevant, engaging, and effective.

In this chapter, we're going to break down the essentials of creating visual content that resonates with your audience, including how to select images, create videos, and leverage graphics to enhance your message.

Image Selection: Choose Wisely, Choose Right

Before you go grabbing any image that seems to fit, let's take a step back. **Not all images are created equal**. In fact, some can do more harm than good. Here's how to select the right image:

1. **High-Quality Images Matter**: Low-resolution images can make your brand look unprofessional. It's like showing up to a party in pajamas when everyone else is in fancy clothes—it just doesn't fit. Always opt for high-quality images that are sharp, clear, and professionally shot. Grainy or pixelated visuals will undermine your credibility.

2. **Relevant Images**: Don't just slap any random image onto your post and call it a day. The image should support the content and message you're conveying. For example, if you're writing a blog post about yoga for beginners, an image of someone struggling with advanced poses won't be helpful. Instead, opt for images that represent your audience's journey and connect with them emotionally.

3. **Authenticity Over Generic Stock Photos**: We've all seen them—the overly posed stock photos with people laughing awkwardly at a computer or shaking hands like they're auditioning for a commercial. These can feel disingenuous and off-putting. **Authentic, real-life images** of people using your products or engaging with your brand resonate better. If possible, use your own photos or hire a photographer who can capture real moments that reflect your brand's values.

4. **Consistent Style**: The images you choose should align with your overall brand aesthetic. This includes factors like color scheme, tone, and subject matter. Consistency across your visuals makes your brand more recognizable and helps build trust with your audience.

Common sense tip: Don't settle for the first image you find. Make sure it adds value and matches your brand's voice. It's better to post fewer, high-quality images than to flood your feed with mediocre ones.

Video Content: The Secret to Engaging Your Audience

Now, let's talk about video. If a picture is worth a thousand words, then video is worth a million. Video content is one of the most engaging forms of media, with the power to convey emotion, information, and brand personality in a way that text and images alone can't. But before you go creating a viral video (or trying to), let's break down some key video best practices.

1. **Keep It Short and Sweet**: You've probably heard that attention spans are shrinking. That's not just a myth—people are less likely to watch long videos all the way through. Aim to keep your videos concise. Short-form videos, like those on Instagram Reels or TikTok, are gaining massive traction. Try to get your point across in 30-60 seconds. Longer videos? Make sure they're packed with value, whether that's through educational content, storytelling, or entertainment.

2. **Value First, Sales Second**: The goal of your video should be to provide value to your audience first and foremost. While it's tempting to make a sales pitch in every video, **audiences can smell a salesy video from a mile away**. Instead, aim to entertain, educate, or inspire. When people feel like they're getting something valuable, they're more likely to trust your brand and convert later on.

3. **Tell a Story**: People love stories. Why do you think we spend hours binge-watching Netflix series? Storytelling helps you create an emotional connection with your audience. Whether it's a customer success story, a behind-the-scenes glimpse of your company, or a tutorial that solves a problem, make sure your video tells

a story that aligns with your brand values.

4. **Add Subtitles**: Did you know that over 80% of videos on social media are watched without sound? That means if you don't add subtitles, you could be missing out on a huge chunk of your audience. Subtitles not only make your video more accessible but also improve engagement, as users can follow along even when they're in a noisy environment or don't have their sound on.

Common sense tip: Keep videos short and focused. Focus on delivering value, and use storytelling to create an emotional connection. And don't forget to add subtitles!

The Power of Infographics and Graphics

Sometimes, the best way to convey complex information is through **infographics**. Infographics are a visual representation of data, statistics, or processes. They break down complex concepts into digestible chunks, making it easier for your audience to understand and retain information.

1. **Use Simple, Clean Designs**: Infographics should be easy to read and visually appealing. Avoid cluttering your graphic with too much text or too many colors. A simple, clean design with a clear flow of information will be more effective.

2. **Highlight Key Information**: Your infographic should prioritize the most important information. Use bold fonts, contrasting colors, and icons to highlight key points and make the information pop.

3. **Data-Driven and Accurate**: Infographics are often used to present statistics or data, so accuracy is key. Always double-check your numbers and sources

before publishing. Providing incorrect information can seriously harm your credibility.

4. **Shareable**: One of the greatest benefits of infographics is their shareability. People love to share helpful, insightful, or funny infographics on social media. When creating infographics, consider how they might be shared and make them easy to save or share with others.

Common sense tip: Infographics can make complex data digestible, but they need to be clear, accurate, and visually balanced. Focus on presenting the key points without overwhelming your audience.

Designing Graphics for Social Media

When it comes to social media, **graphics are king**. Whether it's a quote card, a promotional graphic, or a simple announcement, eye-catching visuals can make a huge difference in how your content is received.

1. **Platform-Specific Design**: Different platforms have different design requirements. For example, Instagram thrives on square images, while Facebook and Twitter are better suited for landscape designs. Always design with the platform in mind to maximize engagement.

2. **Branding**: Ensure that your visuals reflect your brand's personality. Use your brand colors, fonts, and logo consistently across your graphics. This helps build brand recognition and keeps your messaging consistent.

3. **Simplicity is Key**: Overly complicated graphics can confuse your audience. Keep your design simple and direct, especially when it comes to social media posts. Your audience should be able to understand the message in a split second.

Common sense tip: Keep graphics simple, consistent, and tailored to the platform. Make sure your brand's personality shines through in every post.

Conclusion: Visual Content Is Your Secret Weapon

Visual content isn't just about looking pretty—it's about enhancing your message and making it more accessible, engaging, and shareable. Whether you're selecting the right image, creating a short-form video, designing an infographic, or crafting a social media graphic, make sure your visuals are high-quality, relevant, and aligned with your brand.

In the next chapter, we'll dive into **SEO and Content Strategy**, and how optimizing your content can make sure all of your hard work doesn't go unnoticed. Because let's face it—what good is great content if no one can find it?

CHAPTER 7: SOCIAL MEDIA MANAGEMENT WITH COMMON SENSE

When it comes to digital marketing, **social media** is the shining star. It's where your audience hangs out, it's where trends are born, and it's where brands can connect with customers in a real and personal way. But managing social media is a whole different beast. It's not just about posting pretty pictures and waiting for the likes to roll in. It requires strategy, consistency, and a good dose of common sense to navigate through the noise.

In this chapter, we're going to tackle social media management like a pro, with a no-nonsense approach that ensures your social media efforts are effective and aligned with your business goals.

Platform-Specific Strategies: Tailor Your Approach

Just like no two people are exactly alike, **no two social media platforms are the same**. Each platform has its unique vibe, audience, and best practices. So, if you're treating Twitter like Instagram or LinkedIn like Facebook, you're in for a social media disaster.

Here's how to approach different platforms with common sense:

1. **Instagram**: Instagram is the land of visuals, so let your photos and videos speak for themselves. Focus on eye-catching content that tells a story through beautiful imagery, whether it's user-generated content, product

photos, or lifestyle shots. Be consistent with your posts, and leverage Instagram Stories and Reels to stay top of mind. Hashtags are your best friend, but don't overdo it —use relevant hashtags that are actually being searched by your audience.

2. **Facebook**: Facebook is more community-driven and conversational. It's not just about posting content; it's about engaging with your audience. Share a mix of content types: videos, articles, customer reviews, and even polls or quizzes. Take time to respond to comments and messages—social media is all about building relationships. And don't forget to take advantage of Facebook Groups, where you can build a community around your brand.

3. **Twitter**: Twitter is all about being quick, witty, and to the point. Your posts should be concise (no surprise there, given Twitter's character limit), but impactful. Trending topics are an excellent way to get in front of a broader audience, so make sure to stay on top of the latest hashtags and news. Twitter is also a great place to engage with your followers directly—answer questions, join conversations, or even share some humor to connect on a more human level.

4. **LinkedIn**: LinkedIn is the professional network, so it's where your brand can build credibility and authority. Share insightful articles, case studies, or industry news to position yourself as a thought leader. Don't be overly promotional—LinkedIn users are there to connect and learn, not to be sold to. Focus on providing value and making professional connections.

5. **TikTok**: TikTok is all about creativity and entertainment. The key to success here is jumping on

trends and making your content fun, authentic, and easily shareable. Whether it's a behind-the-scenes look at your business, a tutorial, or a viral challenge, TikTok thrives on creativity and personality. Don't take yourself too seriously—TikTok users love relatable, lighthearted content.

Common sense tip: Each platform has its unique characteristics, so customize your content and tone to fit the platform. You can't just copy-paste content and expect it to work everywhere.

Timing and Frequency: Post Like a Pro

You know how annoying it is when your favorite brand posts at 2 AM, and you miss it? Well, your audience feels the same way if you're not posting at the right times. **Timing is everything** in social media. If you want your posts to get the engagement they deserve, you need to post when your audience is most active.

But here's the catch: there's no one-size-fits-all answer. The best times to post vary depending on your audience, location, and the platform. So, while general guidelines might suggest posting in the early morning or late evening, the **real secret** is knowing your audience's habits.

Here's how you can figure that out:

1. **Analyze Your Audience**: Use analytics tools like Facebook Insights, Instagram Insights, or Twitter Analytics to find out when your audience is most active. Check out the data and see if there are any clear patterns in terms of when they engage with your posts.

2. **Experiment**: Test out different posting times and see which ones generate the most engagement. You might discover that your audience is more active in the middle of the afternoon on weekdays, or that evenings are better for weekend posts. **Don't be afraid to experiment**

—data is your best friend.

3. **Consistency**: Posting once a week might not cut it in the fast-paced world of social media. To stay relevant and visible, you need to post consistently. **However**, don't overwhelm your followers with too many posts in a day. Find the sweet spot for your audience—whether that's posting once a day, three times a week, or even a few times a month. Just make sure you stick to it!

Common sense tip: Be mindful of the timing and frequency of your posts, but don't get too obsessed with perfection. Your audience will engage with content that feels timely, relevant, and authentic.

Engaging with the Community: It's Not Just About You

It's easy to get caught up in creating content and hitting "publish," but social media is all about **building relationships**. To truly succeed, you need to engage with your audience in a way that feels genuine. Respond to comments, answer questions, and join conversations. Social media is a two-way street—it's not just about talking at your followers, but talking **with** them.

1. **Responding Promptly**: In today's fast-paced world, people expect quick responses. Whether someone is leaving a comment or sending you a direct message, try to respond in a timely manner. It shows your audience that you care and are actively listening to their feedback.

2. **Encouraging Conversations**: Don't just post content— ask questions, run polls, and create opportunities for your audience to engage. This makes your followers feel like they are part of your brand's community. The more they engage, the more likely they are to stay loyal.

3. **Handling Negative Comments**: Not every comment will

be a love letter. Sometimes, you'll get a complaint or a negative review. Here's the thing: **How you respond to negative feedback can make or break your brand**. Handle it with grace, empathy, and professionalism. Show that you're listening, that you care about resolving the issue, and that you value your customers' opinions.

4. **User-Generated Content (UGC)**: One of the best ways to engage with your community is to feature user-generated content. Encourage your followers to share their experiences with your brand and repost their content. This not only builds trust, but it also shows that you value your community.

Common sense tip: Engaging with your community is about building trust and fostering a sense of belonging. Don't just talk at them—talk **with** them and show them that you care.

Conclusion: Social Media Management is a Marathon, Not a Sprint

Social media management is an ongoing process, and success doesn't happen overnight. It takes time, effort, and a solid strategy. But with a little common sense, you can create a social media presence that not only resonates with your audience but also drives meaningful results.

In the next chapter, we'll dive into **SEO and Content Strategy**, which will show you how to make sure that all of your hard work on social media doesn't go to waste. After all, what good is a killer post if nobody sees it?

Common sense tip for social media: It's about strategy, consistency, and engagement. Make your content fit the platform, post when your audience is active, and always be ready to engage with your community.

CHAPTER 8: MASTERING SEO AND CONTENT STRATEGY

When it comes to digital marketing, SEO (Search Engine Optimization) and content strategy are the dynamic duo that can make or break your efforts. You could create the most beautiful, engaging website or social media post, but if people can't find it, then what's the point? This chapter will help you understand the basics of SEO and content strategy, and how to apply common sense to make sure your content reaches the right audience at the right time.

On-Page Optimization: Making Your Content Search-Friendly

Search engines like Google are constantly crawling the web to index content. When someone types a query into the search bar, Google and other search engines want to provide the most relevant results. On-page SEO is about ensuring your content is structured in a way that search engines can easily understand and rank.

Here's a breakdown of key on-page elements:

1. **Meta Titles and Descriptions**: The meta title and description are the first things people see when they search for something online. Make sure they are **concise, clear**, and contain the main keyword you're targeting. The title should be around 60 characters, and the description should be under 160 characters. These

should describe what your page is about and entice people to click. But don't overstuff them with keywords —focus on being **informative and natural**.

2. **Headers and Subheaders**: Google loves organized content. Use headings (H1, H2, H3, etc.) to break up your content and make it easier to read. Not only does this improve the user experience, but it also helps search engines understand the structure of your page. Your main heading (H1) should include your primary keyword and clearly convey the purpose of the page.

3. **Alt Text for Images**: Search engines can't "see" images, but they can read the **alt text** you attach to them. Alt text is a description of what the image is about, and it helps search engines understand how your visual content fits into the page. This is also crucial for accessibility, as visually impaired users rely on screen readers to interpret alt text.

4. **URL Structure**: Your URLs should be clean, simple, and keyword-rich. A URL like "/products/red-widgets" is far better than "/product12345" because it tells both users and search engines what the page is about.

5. **Internal Linking**: Internal links are links that point to other pages on your own website. They help distribute link equity across your site and allow users to easily navigate related content. Internal linking also keeps visitors engaged longer, reducing bounce rates.

Common sense tip: Think about your audience when you optimize for SEO. Use natural, readable content that aligns with how people actually search.

High-Quality Content: The Heart of Your SEO Strategy

When it comes to SEO, **content is king**. But not just any content —high-quality content. That means writing content that is valuable, engaging, and relevant to your audience. Google rewards websites that provide useful, original content that answers people's questions.

Here's how to create content that works:

1. **Write for Your Audience, Not Just Search Engines**: It's tempting to over-optimize your content for search engines, but remember, **people are your real audience**. Your content should answer their questions, solve their problems, and add value to their lives. Focus on providing solutions, insights, and useful information.

2. **Be Authentic**: Google can spot low-quality, spammy content from a mile away. Content that is stuffed with keywords or written just to rank will hurt your SEO efforts. Focus on **authenticity**. Create content that resonates with your audience and reflects your brand's personality.

3. **Long-Form Content**: Long-form content (over 1,000 words) often performs better in search rankings. Why? Because it typically provides more in-depth answers to people's questions and includes more relevant keywords. But don't make the mistake of writing long content just for the sake of it. Ensure that every word adds value.

4. **Answer the Questions People Are Asking**: One way to boost your content's relevance is by addressing **common questions** within your industry. Use tools like Answer the Public or Google's "People Also Ask" section to find out what people are searching for and create content that answers those questions.

5. **Use Visuals**: Break up long blocks of text with relevant images, infographics, and videos. Not only does this improve user engagement, but it can also boost your rankings—Google values multimedia content, especially video.

Common sense tip: Your content should be created with the audience in mind, not just algorithms. Quality matters more than quantity, and if it's valuable, people will engage with it.

Link Building: Earning Trust

When it comes to SEO, backlinks (links from other websites to yours) are one of the most important ranking factors. Backlinks signal to Google that your content is trustworthy, authoritative, and worth sharing. But **quality matters more than quantity**.

Here's how to build backlinks without resorting to shady tactics:

1. **Guest Blogging**: Write guest posts for reputable blogs in your industry. In exchange for providing high-quality content, you can often include a backlink to your website. Make sure the blog you're writing for has a solid reputation—Google will give more weight to backlinks from authoritative sites.

2. **Create Shareable Content**: The more people share your content, the more likely you are to earn backlinks. Create something people will want to link to—whether that's an insightful blog post, a helpful guide, or a compelling infographic.

3. **Build Relationships with Influencers**: Networking with influencers or thought leaders in your industry can lead to valuable backlinks. Engaging with them on social media or collaborating on projects can help you earn

their trust and, eventually, a link to your content.

4. **Broken Link Building**: This is a clever tactic where you find broken links on other websites and suggest your own content as a replacement. It's a win-win: the website owner gets a working link, and you get a backlink to your site.

Common sense tip: Focus on earning backlinks from reputable, relevant sources. Don't waste your time or money on link schemes or irrelevant links that could harm your SEO efforts.

Content Strategy: Aligning Your Goals with Your Audience's Needs

An effective content strategy goes beyond just writing good content. It involves planning, consistency, and ensuring that everything you create aligns with your business goals. Here's how to build a content strategy that works:

1. **Set Clear Objectives**: Before you start creating content, ask yourself, "What do I want to achieve?" Are you trying to drive traffic, generate leads, or build brand awareness? Having clear goals will help you focus your efforts and measure your success.

2. **Understand Your Audience**: Know who you're creating content for. Understand their pain points, challenges, and interests. Tailor your content to meet their needs. A deep understanding of your audience will help you create content that resonates and drives results.

3. **Content Calendar**: Stay organized by creating a content calendar. This helps you plan your content in advance, ensuring that you stay consistent and that your content supports your overall marketing strategy. A content calendar also helps you avoid the dreaded "What do I

post today?" dilemma.

4. **Repurpose Content**: Not every piece of content needs to be completely new. Repurpose your existing content into different formats. For example, you can turn a blog post into an infographic, a video, or a podcast episode. This way, you get more mileage out of the content you've already created.

5. **Measure and Refine**: Your content strategy isn't set in stone. It's important to measure the performance of your content regularly and refine your strategy as needed. Look at metrics like page views, engagement rates, and conversions to see what's working and what's not.

Common sense tip: Don't overcomplicate your content strategy. Keep it simple, stay focused on your audience, and consistently create content that adds value.

Conclusion: SEO and Content Strategy—The Power Couple

In digital marketing, SEO and content strategy go hand in hand. By optimizing your content for search engines and ensuring it's high-quality, valuable, and aligned with your business goals, you'll increase your chances of success. SEO and content strategy aren't quick fixes—they take time, effort, and consistency. But with a little common sense, you'll be able to create content that not only ranks well but resonates with your audience and drives meaningful results.

In the next chapter, we'll dive into **Paid Advertising Done Right**, where we'll explore how to craft advertising campaigns that actually deliver ROI—without throwing your money down the drain.

CHAPTER 9: PAID ADVERTISING DONE RIGHT

Ah, paid advertising. The golden child of instant traffic and lead generation. While SEO and organic content take time to yield results, paid ads can catapult you to the top of search results or social media feeds with just a few clicks and a budget. But before you pour your hard-earned cash into ads, it's crucial to understand how to use them wisely. The goal is not to spend for the sake of spending but to drive results that make your investment worthwhile.

In this chapter, we'll explore how to use common sense to master paid advertising. We'll cover the nuts and bolts of creating successful ads, setting goals, targeting the right audience, and optimizing your campaigns to ensure you get the most bang for your buck. So, let's dive in and make sure you're not just "throwing money at the wall" with your ads.

Setting Clear Goals: Know What You're Trying to Achieve

The first thing you need to do before creating any paid advertising campaign is to define what success looks like. **Clear, measurable goals** are essential to ensure that your campaigns deliver the results you want.

Here are some common advertising objectives to consider:

1. **Brand Awareness**: If you're looking to introduce your

brand to a larger audience or gain visibility, brand awareness campaigns are a great way to go. The goal here is to get your message in front of as many people as possible, even if they don't take action immediately.

2. **Lead Generation**: If you want to capture email addresses, phone numbers, or other contact information, then lead generation ads are what you're after. These ads often include forms that users can fill out directly within the ad platform (like Facebook or LinkedIn), making it easier for them to take action.

3. **Website Traffic**: If your goal is to drive visitors to your website, then you should optimize your ads to focus on traffic. This is typically a good choice if you have valuable content like blog posts, resources, or landing pages that you want to promote.

4. **Sales and Conversions**: The holy grail of paid ads—sales! If your objective is to drive purchases or other conversions (like sign-ups), you need to optimize your ads for high intent. This might include dynamic retargeting ads or search ads that show up when someone is already searching for products like yours.

Common sense tip: Be specific about your goals. Don't just say, "I want to make more money." Ask yourself, "What do I need to do to make more money?" The more precise your goals, the easier it is to track and measure success.

Targeting the Right Audience: Speak to the People Who Care

One of the most powerful features of paid advertising is the ability to **target specific audiences**. With platforms like Google Ads, Facebook, LinkedIn, and Instagram, you can choose who sees your ads based on criteria like demographics, interests, behaviors, location, and more.

But here's the thing—**don't waste your money targeting everyone**. The more specific you get, the better your ads will perform. Here's how to fine-tune your targeting:

1. **Demographic Targeting**: Demographics are the basic characteristics of your audience, like age, gender, education, and occupation. For instance, if you sell high-end skincare products, you might target women ages 25–45 who have an interest in beauty and wellness.

2. **Interest-Based Targeting**: On platforms like Facebook and Instagram, you can target users based on their interests, hobbies, and past behavior. This is useful if you want to reach people who have shown interest in topics related to your product or service. For example, if you're promoting a fitness app, you can target users who are interested in health, fitness, or weight loss.

3. **Behavioral Targeting**: This involves targeting people based on their past online behavior, like whether they've visited your website, interacted with your content, or made a purchase. Retargeting is a great way to reach people who have already shown interest in your product or service.

4. **Geographic Targeting**: If you run a local business or offer a location-specific product, geo-targeting is essential. Platforms like Google Ads and Facebook let you target users based on their location, whether it's by city, region, or even a specific radius around your business.

Common sense tip: Be realistic about who your ideal customer is. Just because an audience is large doesn't mean it's the right audience. Narrowing your focus will help you get better results and avoid wasting ad spend on people who aren't likely to convert.

Crafting High-Impact Ads: Less Is More

The quality of your ad content plays a huge role in its success. Your ad copy, images, and calls to action (CTAs) need to be compelling enough to get people to stop scrolling and take action. The key is **simplicity**. Here's how to create ads that grab attention:

1. **Clear, Concise Copy**: People have short attention spans, especially on social media. Your ad copy should be direct and easy to understand. Focus on the benefit of your product or service, not just the features. Instead of saying, "Our software includes a variety of features," say, "Save time and boost productivity with our all-in-one software solution."

2. **Engaging Visuals**: Your visuals (images or videos) should be high-quality and relevant to the ad. If your goal is to drive sales, show the product in action. If you're promoting a service, use an image that conveys the outcome the customer will get. And please, no generic stock photos. People can spot them from a mile away.

3. **Strong Call-to-Action (CTA)**: The CTA is the part of your ad that tells people what to do next. It should be **clear, action-oriented**, and make people feel like they can't pass up the opportunity. Examples include "Shop Now," "Learn More," "Sign Up Today," or "Get Started."

4. **Test Variations**: A/B testing (also known as split testing) is a powerful tool that allows you to experiment with different versions of your ads to see which one performs better. You can test different headlines, images, CTAs, and more to find the combination that

works best.

Common sense tip: Keep your ads simple and focused. The less fluff, the better. If you're trying to convey too much information, people will tune out.

A/B Testing: The Key to Continuous Improvement

You've launched your ad, and you're waiting for results. But what if the first version doesn't perform as well as you hoped? That's where **A/B testing** comes in. A/B testing involves running multiple variations of the same ad and comparing their performance.

Here's how to do it effectively:

1. **Test One Element at a Time**: For accurate results, test only one element of the ad at a time. For example, you could test two different CTAs to see which one drives more clicks. If you test the copy, images, and CTA all at once, you won't know which factor influenced the results.

2. **Track Key Metrics**: Measure the metrics that matter most to your campaign goals. For example, if you're trying to generate leads, track conversion rates. If you're focused on sales, monitor return on ad spend (ROAS).

3. **Optimize Based on Results**: Once you've tested different versions of your ad, optimize your campaigns by using the winning variations. Don't be afraid to tweak your ads periodically to improve performance.

Common sense tip: A/B testing isn't just for newbies—it's an ongoing process. Even when you think you've found the perfect ad, testing can help you refine it even further.

Conclusion: Paid Advertising—The Smart Way

Paid advertising can be a game-changer for your business if you do it right. But remember, success isn't about throwing money at ads and hoping for the best. It's about setting clear goals, targeting the right audience, crafting impactful ads, and constantly optimizing. With a little common sense and strategic planning, paid advertising can help you achieve measurable results and maximize your return on investment.

In the next chapter, we'll dive into **Analytics and Reporting**, where we'll discuss how to turn all the data from your campaigns into actionable insights that can guide your future marketing efforts.

CHAPTER 10: ANALYTICS AND REPORTING

So, you've launched your digital marketing campaigns, you've spent some budget on ads, created content, and maybe even sent out a few emails. Now what? If you're like most marketers, you're probably staring at a pile of data, wondering, "How do I make sense of all this?" Welcome to the world of analytics and reporting—the place where raw numbers and metrics transform into valuable insights.

In this chapter, we'll dive into the wonderful world of analytics, helping you decipher the data and turn it into actionable steps that will improve your future campaigns. The key is to **focus on what matters**—not every metric is worth chasing. We'll also talk about the importance of setting up proper reporting systems so that you can keep track of your performance and optimize your strategies over time.

Common sense tip: Analytics isn't just about tracking everything —it's about tracking the right things. So let's cut through the noise and figure out what really matters.

Turning Data Into Action: The Essentials of Marketing Metrics

When it comes to digital marketing, there's no shortage of numbers to keep an eye on. From click-through rates (CTR) to bounce rates to conversion rates, it's easy to get overwhelmed. However, just because there's a lot of data doesn't mean all of it is useful. In fact, some metrics are **vanity metrics**—they look good on paper but don't actually tell you much about whether your campaigns are successful.

Here's a quick guide to help you distinguish between metrics that matter and those that don't:

1. **Conversion Rate**: This is one of the most important metrics to track. It's the percentage of people who complete the desired action (like making a purchase, signing up for a newsletter, etc.) after clicking on your ad or landing page. A low conversion rate might mean your landing page or ad needs optimization.

2. **Click-Through Rate (CTR)**: CTR measures how often people click on your ad after seeing it. It's an important metric to track because it tells you whether your ad copy and visuals are compelling enough to prompt action. A low CTR might indicate that your ad isn't resonating with your audience.

3. **Return on Investment (ROI)**: This metric tells you whether your marketing efforts are making you money. It's calculated by subtracting the total cost of your campaign from the revenue generated, then dividing by the cost. If your ROI is positive, great! If not, you may need to rethink your strategy.

4. **Bounce Rate**: Bounce rate measures how many people leave your website without taking any further action. A high bounce rate can indicate that your website isn't engaging visitors, or that your landing page isn't aligned with the ad or content that led them there. A well-designed, user-friendly website can lower your bounce rate.

5. **Customer Acquisition Cost (CAC)**: This is how much it

costs to acquire a new customer. It includes everything from paid ads to the time spent on your content marketing efforts. By measuring your CAC, you can determine whether your marketing strategy is cost-effective.

6. **Engagement Rate**: This is an essential metric for social media campaigns. It includes likes, comments, shares, and other forms of interaction. A high engagement rate means that people are connecting with your content, which is a good sign that you're on the right track.

Common sense tip: Focus on the metrics that directly align with your goals. If you're aiming for conversions, metrics like CTR and conversion rate should be your primary focus. Don't get distracted by metrics that don't drive business results.

Setting Up Your Analytics: Tools You Need to Track Success

Tracking and analyzing data would be nearly impossible without the right tools. Fortunately, there are many powerful analytics platforms out there that can help you monitor performance, track metrics, and generate reports. Here are some of the most popular and useful tools for digital marketers:

1. **Google Analytics**: Google Analytics is an absolute must for tracking website traffic and user behavior. It provides data on how people interact with your website, where they're coming from, and what pages they're visiting. You can also set up goals (such as form submissions or purchases) to track conversions.

2. **Google Ads**: If you're running paid ads through Google, Google Ads' reporting tools give you valuable insights into campaign performance, keyword performance, and return on ad spend (ROAS). It's crucial to regularly monitor this data to tweak your campaigns for better

performance.

3. **Facebook Insights**: If you're running Facebook or Instagram ads, Facebook's Insights tool provides a wealth of data on how your posts and ads are performing. It shows you who's engaging with your content, how often they're engaging, and which types of posts get the most attention.

4. **HubSpot**: HubSpot is a comprehensive marketing and CRM platform that includes analytics features for tracking website performance, lead generation, social media engagement, and more. It's great for marketers who want an all-in-one solution for managing and reporting on their campaigns.

5. **Hootsuite or Buffer**: These social media management tools offer built-in analytics features that allow you to track engagement, follower growth, and post-performance across different social media platforms. They also make it easier to schedule and track the success of your posts over time.

Common sense tip: Pick tools that are right for your needs and budget. While it's tempting to use multiple tools for everything, it's more effective to master one or two and use them consistently.

Avoiding Over-Analysis: The Paradox of Too Much Data

While data is essential, there's such a thing as **paralysis by analysis**. Sometimes, marketers get so caught up in tracking every little detail that they end up doing nothing with the insights they gather. Here's how to avoid that trap:

1. **Prioritize Actionable Data**: Focus on the metrics that directly inform your next steps. For instance, if your CTR is low, take action by tweaking your ad copy or

design. If your bounce rate is high, maybe it's time to improve your landing page experience.

2. **Set Time Limits**: It's easy to get caught in a rabbit hole of data analysis. Set a specific time for reviewing your metrics (e.g., once a week or once a month) and stick to it. Don't spend all your time analyzing; instead, use your findings to make adjustments and improve your campaigns.

3. **Don't Sweat the Small Stuff**: Not every small fluctuation in data is worth worrying about. Stay focused on the big picture and the long-term trends. For example, if one ad underperforms slightly on a single day, don't jump to conclusions. Assess performance over time before making major changes.

Common sense tip: Keep it simple. If the data doesn't help you make a better decision or improve your strategy, then it's not worth stressing over.

Reporting: The Final Step

Once you've gathered your data and insights, it's time to present them in a clear, digestible format. That's where **reporting** comes in. A well-structured report is essential for tracking progress, sharing results with stakeholders, and making informed decisions about future campaigns.

Here are a few tips for creating effective marketing reports:

1. **Be Clear and Concise**: Focus on the key metrics that matter most. Don't drown your audience in unnecessary details. Use charts, graphs, and visuals to make the data easy to understand.

2. **Show Trends Over Time**: It's important to show how

your performance is evolving over time. For example, if you're tracking sales, compare data month-over-month or quarter-over-quarter to highlight trends.

3. **Provide Actionable Insights**: Don't just present the numbers—offer insights into what those numbers mean and how they'll impact future strategies. For instance, if your conversion rate is low, suggest A/B testing or landing page improvements as potential solutions.

Common sense tip: Your reports should be a tool for action, not just a collection of data. Make sure your audience knows exactly what the next steps are.

Conclusion: Analytics Is Your Friend, Not Your Foe

Analytics is more than just a bunch of numbers on a screen—it's a powerful tool that helps you understand how your marketing efforts are performing and what you can do to improve them. By tracking the right metrics, using the right tools, and focusing on actionable insights, you can optimize your campaigns and achieve your goals more effectively.

In the next chapter, we'll dive into **Real-World Anecdotes**, where we'll look at some of the mistakes marketers often make, as well as the success stories that prove the value of applying common sense in digital marketing. Stay tuned!

CHAPTER 11: REAL-WORLD ANECDOTES

There's nothing quite like learning from others' successes—and mistakes. While we can discuss theory, strategies, and data all day long, the real value comes when you see how common sense in digital marketing has played out in the real world. In this chapter, we'll share some stories that will make you laugh, cringe, and maybe even inspire you to think a little differently about your own marketing efforts. After all, in digital marketing, no one is immune to making mistakes—but the key is learning from them and improving.

Avoidable Mistakes: What Not to Do

Let's start with the cautionary tales. Every marketer has faced their fair share of embarrassing missteps. The key takeaway here is that most of these mistakes could have been avoided with a little bit of common sense. Take a look at these examples, and see if you can spot where the logical solution was glaringly absent.

Example 1: The Case of the Typos in the High-Budget Campaign

This one comes from a well-known retail brand that decided to run a large, high-budget ad campaign just in time for the holiday shopping season. Everything seemed perfect—except for one thing. In their rush to launch the campaign, someone accidentally left a typo in the headline of the ad. And not just any typo. A glaring one. They wrote "up to 50% off" when it should have been "up to 60% off."

This wasn't just an error—it was a massive mistake. The typo was spotted only after the ad had been live for a full 24 hours, by which point a significant portion of the campaign budget had already been spent. The result? Customers who were interested in the deal felt misled, and the brand lost out on valuable trust and conversions.

The Common Sense Fix: A simple second pair of eyes could have caught this before the ad went live. Whether it's a typo, a broken link, or a misaligned message, always ensure that your content goes through thorough proofreading and review. It's better to take a little extra time than risk a costly blunder.

Example 2: The Holiday Post That Wasn't So Holiday-Appropriate

Here's another real-world example, this time from a popular fast-food chain. They had planned a social media post to celebrate a major holiday, but in their excitement to share the news, they accidentally scheduled the post on the wrong day. To make matters worse, the post was about a promotion that was meant to run only the day before the holiday, and the message was out of sync with the actual holiday celebrations.

The post didn't align with the holiday vibe at all—customers felt like it was a poorly timed sales pitch rather than a genuine celebration. Worse, the social media backlash was immediate, with people mocking the brand for being tone-deaf and out of touch.

The Common Sense Fix: Before scheduling posts, take a moment to ensure the timing makes sense. And for special occasions, make sure your content is in sync with the mood of the event. It's not just about promoting your product—it's about showing that you understand and value the moment.

Success Stories: When Common Sense Wins

Now that we've learned from some mistakes, let's shift gears and highlight some success stories. These are examples where common sense wasn't just useful—it was the secret sauce to creating campaigns that worked.

Example 3: The Local Cafe That Knows Its Community

A local café, known for its freshly brewed coffee and cozy atmosphere, decided to run a social media campaign that showcased their unique customer experience. They didn't use fancy graphics or over-the-top ads—instead, they shared genuine customer stories, highlighting regulars who came in every morning for their daily cup of joe.

The campaign included user-generated content, where the café encouraged customers to share their favorite coffee moments on social media, offering small discounts in return for posts. The response was overwhelming. Customers loved seeing their own stories featured, and the café gained a more engaged and loyal customer base. The campaign was simple, but it worked because it was rooted in authenticity and common sense—no gimmicks, just real people.

The Common Sense Win: This café understood that its best asset was its community. Instead of focusing on high-budget ads or trying to be something it wasn't, it embraced its local identity and created a campaign that resonated on a personal level.

Example 4: The E-Commerce Brand That Understood Timing

An e-commerce company in the fashion industry was running a sale for a popular holiday season. However, instead of bombarding customers with constant reminders of the sale, they decided to use a subtle yet effective strategy. The brand sent out a well-timed email just a few hours before the sale was about to end. They included a simple message with a clear call-to-action and an urgency-driven offer: "Only 3 hours left to get 30% off your favorite items!"

The email had a high conversion rate because it played on the psychology of urgency without feeling like a pushy sales tactic. Customers felt they were getting a good deal without being overwhelmed by constant messages.

The Common Sense Win: The company understood the importance of timing and urgency in digital marketing. They didn't overdo it, and the result was a well-executed, high-converting campaign.

Key Takeaways from Real-World Anecdotes

What can we learn from these stories? Whether you're dealing with a massive campaign or a simple social media post, common sense goes a long way. Here are a few key takeaways:

1. **Proofread everything**: Typos may seem small, but they can have a big impact. Always double-check your content, especially when you're dealing with a high-visibility campaign.

2. **Timing matters**: Whether it's a social media post or a special promotion, make sure the timing aligns with the occasion or the intended message. A post meant for a holiday should feel festive, not like a random sales pitch.

3. **Stay authentic**: Don't overcomplicate things. When you focus on what your audience values, you're more likely to create campaigns that feel genuine and resonate on a personal level.

4. **Embrace simplicity**: The most successful campaigns often aren't the most complicated ones. Simplicity, clarity, and a little bit of common sense go a long way in cutting through the digital noise.

Conclusion: Learning from Mistakes and Celebrating Wins

Digital marketing doesn't come with a foolproof manual. It's a blend of creativity, strategy, and a healthy dose of trial and error. But when you apply common sense, the chances of avoiding costly mistakes—and creating campaigns that truly connect with your audience—skyrocket.

In the next chapter, we'll dive into **Conclusion: The Takeaway**, where we'll wrap up everything we've learned in this book and leave you with actionable steps to implement common sense in every part of your digital marketing strategy. You're now equipped to create smarter, more effective campaigns that will not only deliver results but also build trust with your audience. Keep it simple, keep it smart, and most importantly, keep it real.

CHAPTER 12: THE FUTURE OF DIGITAL MARKETING

The future of digital marketing is a thrilling mix of technology, data, and creativity. Artificial Intelligence (AI) is making waves across industries, and marketing is no exception. From personalized content to automated customer service, AI is revolutionizing the way we connect with audiences. But while AI might seem like the new star of the digital marketing world, there's one thing that will never go out of style—common sense.

In this chapter, we'll explore how AI will reshape digital marketing and why combining the power of AI with a healthy dose of common sense is the ultimate recipe for success.

AI: The Game Changer in Digital Marketing

Let's face it: marketing today is data-driven. Every click, search, and interaction generates an endless stream of data, and AI is uniquely suited to process and make sense of it all. But what does that mean for digital marketers?

1. Predictive Analytics and Personalization

AI is fantastic at analyzing massive amounts of data to identify trends and predict future behavior. By using AI, marketers can create highly personalized experiences for customers, offering them products or services tailored to their unique needs and preferences.

For instance, AI can track how customers engage with websites and social media platforms, then use that data to serve up personalized ads, content, or product recommendations. This is not only more efficient than traditional methods, but it also helps to increase customer satisfaction and conversion rates. Imagine sending a customer an email with a product they were eyeing a few days ago but didn't purchase. It's like reading their mind, and AI can make that happen.

Common Sense Tip: While personalization is powerful, it's important not to cross the line into creepy territory. Bombarding users with overly personalized messages, especially when they haven't interacted with your brand in a while, can lead to annoyance. The key is to strike a balance—offer personalization, but don't overdo it. Keep it relevant and respectful.

2. AI-Powered Chatbots and Customer Service

We've all interacted with chatbots at some point, whether it's asking about product availability or troubleshooting an issue. AI-powered chatbots are becoming more sophisticated by the day, able to handle everything from basic customer service inquiries to more complex problems, all without human intervention.

These bots can provide instant, 24/7 customer support, significantly improving response time and customer satisfaction. They can also gather valuable data from customer interactions, which can then be used to improve future marketing strategies. What's not to love about AI stepping in to improve efficiency and cut down on human error?

Common Sense Tip: While AI chatbots are great, there's no substitute for human empathy. Make sure your chatbot knows when to escalate to a live agent for situations that require a personal touch. After all, no bot can replace a human connection when it comes to sensitive or complicated issues.

3. Automated Content Creation

AI is also stepping into the realm of content creation. From generating product descriptions to writing blog posts and social media captions, AI can now produce content that reads naturally and engages audiences. Tools like GPT-3 (the technology behind this very conversation) can write articles, create video scripts, and even craft ad copy.

While AI-generated content can be a real time-saver, it's important to remember that it's still far from perfect. The tone, context, and emotional depth of content are areas where AI can sometimes fall short. And let's face it: robots aren't known for their humor, wit, or charm.

Common Sense Tip: Use AI-generated content as a tool, not a crutch. AI is great for producing basic content or scaling up your efforts, but you should always review and refine what's been generated. Infuse your unique voice, humor, and creativity into the content to ensure it truly resonates with your audience.

4. AI in Ad Campaigns: Smarter Spending

Gone are the days of guessing which audience segment to target or how to allocate your budget across multiple platforms. AI can analyze ad performance in real-time, make adjustments, and even predict the best times to run campaigns. Whether it's adjusting bids in a pay-per-click (PPC) campaign or optimizing ad creatives, AI can help digital marketers get the most bang for their buck.

AI can also help identify the most effective channels and customer segments, ensuring that ad spend is allocated efficiently. For instance, AI can determine which demographic is most likely to convert on a particular ad, allowing marketers to adjust their targeting and messaging accordingly.

Common Sense Tip: While AI can optimize your ad campaigns, it's still important to understand your audience on a human level. Make sure your ads are not just data-driven but also resonate emotionally with your target market. Data is important, but context and creativity will always play a key role in crafting compelling campaigns.

Why Common Sense Will Always Be the Secret Sauce

As powerful as AI is, it's not foolproof. AI algorithms rely on data, and data isn't always perfect. You've heard the saying "garbage in, garbage out," right? Well, AI is only as good as the data it receives. That's where common sense comes in.

AI can process vast amounts of data and optimize strategies, but it lacks the ability to understand nuance, empathy, and the bigger picture in the way humans can. Common sense is what gives you the ability to step back and ask, "Does this really make sense for my audience?" or "What's the potential fallout from this decision?"

AI might tell you to target a specific demographic because the data suggests they're more likely to convert, but common sense will tell you that your product might not resonate with them as strongly as you think. AI might recommend a campaign that's optimized for high traffic, but common sense will remind you that the quality of traffic—i.e., customers who are genuinely interested in your product—is just as important as the volume.

The Role of Creativity in an AI-Driven World

As AI continues to advance, one of the biggest concerns in digital marketing is the potential for creativity to take a backseat to automation. After all, if AI can churn out thousands of pieces of content, manage ads, and even handle customer service, what's left for humans to do?

Here's the thing: while AI can handle the repetitive tasks, it's human creativity that adds the spark. No algorithm can replicate the ingenuity of a fresh idea, the subtlety of a well-crafted story, or the emotional connection that a brand can forge with its audience.

Common Sense Tip: Don't let AI replace the creative process. Use it as a tool to enhance your creativity, not as a replacement for it. AI can handle the data and optimization, but it's your vision and ideas that will make your brand stand out.

Conclusion: AI and Common Sense – A Perfect Partnership

AI is changing the face of digital marketing, making it smarter, more efficient, and more personalized than ever before. But the best results come when AI is paired with human insight, empathy, and, yes, common sense. As we move into the future, digital marketers must learn to embrace both the power of AI and the timeless value of human judgment.

AI will do its part, but common sense will always be the secret ingredient that makes sure everything works together seamlessly. After all, at the end of the day, it's not just about the data or the algorithms—it's about understanding your audience and making decisions that feel human, relatable, and authentic.

CHAPTER 13: A MESSAGE TO DIGITAL MARKETING EXECUTIVES AND FREELANCERS

As digital marketing continues to evolve, the landscape can sometimes feel overwhelming. With new technologies, strategies, and trends emerging almost daily, it's easy to lose sight of the one thing that truly makes a difference: common sense.

Whether you're a digital marketing executive working at an agency, a freelancer managing your own clients, or someone just starting out in the industry, this chapter is for you. In this section, we'll explore the unique challenges and opportunities that digital marketing professionals face today and discuss how you can thrive by combining the power of data with the wisdom of common sense.

The Changing Role of Digital Marketers

Gone are the days when digital marketing was all about simply running ads and posting on social media. Today, digital marketers are expected to be data scientists, content creators, brand strategists, and customer experience managers—all rolled into one. The tools we use are more sophisticated, the channels more diverse, and the competition fiercer than ever.

As an executive or freelancer, you may find yourself juggling multiple responsibilities, trying to keep up with the latest trends, and constantly learning new skills. This can sometimes feel like drinking from a fire hose, with endless streams of information and technology coming at you from all directions.

But here's the thing: you don't need to be an expert in every tool or trend to succeed. In fact, some of the best marketers today aren't the ones who know everything—they're the ones who know how to use common sense, make smart decisions, and keep things simple when needed.

Embrace the Power of Data, But Don't Let It Control You

We live in a world where data is king. From customer behavior and website analytics to campaign performance metrics, data-driven marketing has become the backbone of modern strategy. AI tools and automation platforms are constantly collecting, analyzing, and presenting data to help marketers make better decisions.

But while data is incredibly valuable, it's important not to let it be the only thing that guides your decisions. Over-reliance on numbers can lead to "analysis paralysis," where you become so focused on optimizing every little detail that you miss the bigger picture.

Here's where common sense comes in. Yes, use data to inform your strategy—but don't let it make every decision for you. If a campaign looks great on paper but doesn't resonate with your audience emotionally, it's not going to succeed, no matter how many metrics tell you it should.

Pro Tip: Look at the data, but trust your instincts and creativity. Sometimes the best marketing ideas come from outside the numbers.

The Importance of Human Connection in an AI World

AI, automation, and machine learning are revolutionizing the marketing landscape. From generating personalized content to optimizing ad spends, AI tools can handle repetitive tasks, analyze vast amounts of data, and even help predict customer behavior.

However, there's one thing that AI will never replace—genuine human connection. In an increasingly digital world, consumers still crave authentic, relatable, and human-driven interactions with brands. As a digital marketer, your job is not just to push products but to build relationships and foster trust.

Whether you're a freelancer crafting a compelling brand story for a client or an executive overseeing a customer service chatbot, always remember that your audience is made up of real people, not just data points. Use AI and automation as tools to enhance your work, but don't lose sight of the human touch that truly makes your brand stand out.

Pro Tip: When creating content or managing campaigns, always ask yourself, "Would a human being connect with this?" If the answer is no, it's time to rethink the approach.

Why Creativity Will Always Be Your Secret Weapon

It's easy to get caught up in the technical aspects of digital marketing—SEO algorithms, Google Analytics, A/B testing, and all the other tools that promise to boost your campaign's performance. While these tools are important, the one thing that will always set you apart is creativity.

At the end of the day, people don't buy from brands—they buy from brands they connect with. And connection is rooted in creativity. Whether it's the way you tell a brand's story, the humor you use in your ad copy, or the unique angle you take with your content, creativity is what makes your marketing memorable.

In a world filled with automation and AI-driven strategies, creativity is your superpower. It's what allows you to break through the noise and capture your audience's attention. So, never underestimate the power of a great idea.

Pro Tip: Don't be afraid to take risks and experiment with new ideas. You'll never know what works until you try. And sometimes, the most unconventional ideas lead to the most successful campaigns.

Balancing Multiple Roles: How to Stay Sane as a Marketer

Whether you're managing campaigns for clients as a freelancer or overseeing a team as an executive, balancing the demands of digital marketing can feel like a full-time juggling act. There's always something new to learn, something to optimize, and another deadline just around the corner.

Here's where common sense is your best friend. Instead of trying to do everything at once, prioritize what matters most and focus on quality over quantity. Set clear goals, break tasks down into manageable chunks, and remember that it's okay to ask for help when you need it.

For freelancers, it's easy to fall into the trap of taking on too many clients or projects, thinking that more work equals more success. But spreading yourself too thin can lead to burnout and lower-quality work. Focus on the clients who align with your expertise and values, and make sure you're delivering the best work possible.

For digital marketing executives, managing a team comes with its own challenges. You need to balance strategic planning with day-to-day execution, all while keeping your team motivated and aligned with your company's goals. As a leader, your common sense will help you guide your team through challenges and avoid burnout.

Pro Tip: Remember to take breaks and recharge. A clear, rested mind is much more effective than a tired one.

The Future of Digital Marketing: Stay Adaptable

The digital marketing landscape is constantly evolving, and so should you. Whether it's keeping up with new social media algorithms, mastering the latest AI tools, or experimenting with new ad formats, staying adaptable is key to long-term success.

That said, adaptability doesn't mean throwing common sense out the window. It means learning new things and embracing change while staying grounded in the basics that matter most —understanding your audience, being authentic, and thinking creatively.

In the coming years, digital marketers will need to navigate even more technological advancements, but the foundation of common sense will continue to be the cornerstone of successful campaigns.

Conclusion: Combining Common Sense with the Future of Marketing

To all the digital marketing executives and freelancers out there: You are at the forefront of an exciting and dynamic field. The future of marketing will be driven by technology, but the human touch will always be essential. As you navigate new tools, trends, and challenges, remember that common sense, creativity, and a genuine connection with your audience will always set you apart.

Keep experimenting, keep learning, and keep pushing the boundaries of what's possible. With the right combination of common sense and innovation, there's no limit to what you can achieve.

CHAPTER 14:
A MESSAGE TO
DIGITAL MARKETING
AGENCY OWNERS

As the owner of a digital marketing agency, you wear many hats. You're not just the boss—you're the strategist, the marketer, the financial planner, the client liaison, and often, the one who holds everything together when things get tough. With the industry evolving at lightning speed, it's easy to get caught up in the whirlwind of trends, tools, and new technologies. However, amidst all this complexity, there's one thing that remains your most powerful asset: **common sense**.

This chapter is dedicated to helping you navigate the often chaotic world of running a digital marketing agency. We'll discuss how to stay grounded in the basics, make wise decisions, and build a sustainable business that thrives in an increasingly competitive market.

Embracing the Foundation: Common Sense as the Cornerstone of Agency Success

Running a digital marketing agency requires more than just a deep understanding of marketing tactics. You need to be able to balance the delicate dance between creativity and data, deliver measurable results, manage client expectations, and keep your team motivated and productive. And most importantly, you need to make sure that your clients feel heard and valued.

While it's easy to get caught up in the excitement of the latest AI tools or social media trends, **common sense** should always be your guiding principle. It's what helps you stay focused on the end goal: achieving real, sustainable results for your clients. Whether you're building a new website, running an ad campaign, or executing an SEO strategy, always remember that **simplicity and logic** often yield the best results.

The Importance of Setting Realistic Expectations with Clients

One of the biggest challenges as an agency owner is managing client expectations. In an age of instant gratification and viral success stories, clients often come to you with high hopes and unrealistic expectations. They want overnight success, and they want it now. It's up to you to help them understand the truth about digital marketing: it's a long game, and sustainable results take time.

Common sense can help you set clear, realistic goals with your clients right from the start. Don't promise what you can't deliver. Instead, educate your clients on the process, and explain that marketing success is built on consistent effort and strategic decision-making. Help them understand the value of long-term strategies such as SEO, content marketing, and relationship building over quick wins that are often unsustainable.

Pro Tip: When onboarding new clients, create clear timelines, deliverables, and performance metrics. This will help you manage expectations and ensure both you and the client are on the same page.

Building a Team That Operates on Common Sense

As an agency owner, one of your most important responsibilities is leading and building a talented team. But here's the catch— having the most talented people isn't always enough. It's critical that your team members not only have the technical expertise but also share a common-sense approach to marketing.

In the rush to adopt new technologies, it's easy to lose sight of the basics. But while automation, AI, and advanced tools can make your team more efficient, they can never replace the human element of marketing. Your team should always ask, "Does this make sense for the client's brand?" before jumping into the latest marketing tactic.

Encourage your team to think strategically, align with your agency's core values, and prioritize the client's needs. Remind them that the end goal is always to drive measurable results —whether that's increasing sales, growing brand awareness, or building customer loyalty.

Pro Tip: Foster a culture of common sense by having regular team discussions about campaign performance, challenges, and improvements. Encourage open dialogue about what worked and what didn't, and learn from both successes and failures.

Balancing Creativity with Practicality

As the leader of a creative agency, you likely deal with a constant influx of fresh, innovative ideas. Creativity is what sets your agency apart and gives your clients a competitive edge. However, there's a fine line between creative ideas that work and those that overcomplicate things.

Common sense tells us that while creativity is crucial, it should always serve a practical purpose. An idea should be valuable, achievable, and aligned with the client's goals. If your team suggests a campaign that's overly complex or doesn't resonate with the target audience, it's time to take a step back and ask: **Does this make sense?**

Pro Tip: Always balance creativity with logic. Test new ideas, but make sure they align with the client's goals and budget. A creative, yet simple solution often works better than a complicated one.

The Power of Process and Consistency

When you're managing multiple clients, campaigns, and projects, it can be easy to lose sight of the importance of consistent processes. However, creating streamlined workflows will not only help your team stay organized, but it will also help ensure that no client is neglected or overlooked.

Common sense tells us that consistency breeds reliability and trust. By implementing a structured process for managing clients, developing campaigns, and tracking performance, you ensure that your agency runs smoothly and that your clients receive the best possible service.

Create clear guidelines for everything—from onboarding new clients and setting up campaigns to tracking results and optimizing strategies. This will not only save time but will also help build credibility with your clients and establish your agency as a reliable partner.

Pro Tip: Use project management tools and software to keep everything organized. This will help you track deadlines, monitor progress, and ensure that all tasks are completed on time.

Managing Finances: Knowing When to Scale and When to Hold Back

Running an agency is not just about delivering outstanding marketing results—it's also about managing your business's finances effectively. One of the biggest challenges that agency owners face is scaling their operations. While growth is important, it's equally important to scale at a sustainable pace.

Common sense dictates that you should not hire more team members or invest in new technologies until you're certain that it's financially viable. Expanding your business too quickly can lead to cash flow problems, burnout, and a dip in quality. Instead, focus on building a solid foundation, optimizing your current processes, and expanding when the time is right.

Pro Tip: Before scaling your agency, take the time to review your finances. Make sure you have the resources to sustain growth and that your agency's operations can handle an increased workload without compromising quality.

The Future of Digital Marketing Agencies: Adapt and Evolve

The digital marketing industry is constantly changing, and as an agency owner, you must be adaptable. New platforms, algorithms, and marketing strategies are always emerging, and it's essential to stay ahead of the curve. But, at the same time, remember that trends come and go. What's truly important is the ability to blend **new techniques with common-sense strategies** that stand the test of time.

As technology continues to evolve, AI, automation, and advanced analytics will become even more integral to the way agencies operate. But don't be tempted to adopt every new trend just because it's the next big thing. Use your experience and common sense to evaluate whether a new tool or strategy will truly benefit your clients or if it's simply a passing fad.

Pro Tip: Keep learning and stay informed about new trends, but don't jump on every new technology or tool. Always ask, "How does this benefit my clients, and is it worth the investment?"

Conclusion: The Common Sense Agency Owner

As the owner of a digital marketing agency, you are the captain of the ship. Your ability to balance creativity with practicality, set realistic expectations with clients, and lead a team grounded in common sense will be the keys to your long-term success.

The world of digital marketing will continue to evolve, and so will your agency. But remember, while new technologies and strategies come and go, **common sense will always be your guiding light**. It's the foundation upon which you can build a successful, sustainable business that delivers real results for your clients.

CONCLUSION: THE POWER OF COMMON SENSE IN DIGITAL MARKETING

As we wrap up this journey through the world of digital marketing, one thing becomes crystal clear: **common sense** is the unsung hero behind every successful campaign. Amid all the fancy buzzwords, complex algorithms, and endless tools at our disposal, it's often the simplest, most practical decisions that deliver the greatest results. From understanding your audience to creating content that resonates, the ability to think logically, empathize with your customers, and stay grounded in real-world scenarios is what separates successful marketers from those chasing the latest trend without real impact.

Digital marketing will continue to evolve, with new technologies, platforms, and strategies emerging all the time. But no matter how sophisticated the tools or the latest AI-driven solution, one thing will remain constant: the need to think critically, communicate effectively, and put the audience first. If you integrate these principles into your work, you'll not only survive the digital marketing jungle—you'll thrive in it.

Whether you're a seasoned professional or a freelancer just starting out, remember that success in digital marketing doesn't require you to know everything—it requires you to make sensible decisions that align with your brand's purpose and connect with your audience. With common sense as your guiding principle, you'll be able to cut through the noise and focus on what truly matters: creating value for your customers and driving meaningful results for your business.

In the end, the goal is simple: **deliver campaigns that work, resonate, and drive action.** And this all starts with applying a little bit of common sense in everything you do.

A WORD ABOUT MAYUR MERAI

Mayur Merai, the author of this book, is a seasoned digital marketing professional and the founder of Social Wits, a digital marketing agency that specializes in helping businesses achieve success through practical, data-driven strategies. With years of experience in the industry, Mayur understands the importance of blending creativity with logic, technology with human-centric thinking, to create campaigns that not only drive traffic but also create lasting relationships with customers.

Having worked with a wide range of clients, from yoga studios to crypto investment projects, Mayur is passionate about demystifying digital marketing and helping others avoid the pitfalls of over-complication. Through this book, he hopes to empower marketers at all levels to approach their campaigns with clarity, purpose, and above all, **common sense**.

Mayur's approach to digital marketing is rooted in the belief that the best strategies are those that are simple, effective, and aligned with the real needs of the audience. He continues to inspire both newcomers and experienced marketers to embrace a practical approach to their work, making digital marketing accessible and enjoyable for everyone.